# To Decorate A Casket

*poems by*

# Bill Ratner

*Finishing Line Press*
Georgetown, Kentucky

# To Decorate A Casket

ACKNOWLEDGMENTS

Thanks to the publishers and editors who have published the following poems:

"Emily" - *Ramingo's Porch*
"Imaginary Ring – *Alta Dena Review*
"Keep Your Eye on the Ball" - *Chiron Review*
"Locker Room Talk" – *Alta Dena Literary Review*
"Mannequin" – *Nixes Mate*
"Milk and Hyacinth" - *Alta Dena Literary Review*
"Mother and Father" - *Uppagus*
"Mr. Death" - *Southern Florida Poetry Journal*
"Phoebe" - *KYSO Flash*
"The Clinic" - *Loch Raven Review*
"Try My Luck" – *Rat's Ass Review*
"Wabash Banner Blue" – *Headstuff*

And thanks to the poets who have taken me in hand and helped me write: Jack
Grapes, Alexis Rhone Fancher, Jill Alexander Essbaum, Carol Frost, Craig Cotter,
Terry Wolverton, Kim Dower, Don Kingfisher Campbell, G.T. Foster, Perie Longo,
Elya Braden, Jacinta White, Kelly Grace Thomas, Tresha Faye Haefner, Mehnaz
Sahibzada, Armine Iknadossian, Mary Wood, Nancy Scherlong, Richard Blanco,
Richard Jones, Jennifer Clement, James Fenton, Rachel Kann, Luis Alberto Urrea.


Publisher: Leah Huete de Maines
Editor: Christen Kincaid
Cover Art: "Voices in my Head," Micah Chambers-Goldberg
Author Photo: Myles Pettengill
Cover Design: Elizabeth Maines McCleavy


Order online: www.finishinglinepress.com
also available on amazon.com

Author inquiries and mail orders:
Finishing Line Press
PO Box 1626
Georgetown, Kentucky 40324
USA

# Table of Contents

**Phoebe**

*Let's select someone from your past,*
the doctor says, *Someone you trusted.*
I line them all up a spray of snapshots
but no one really qualifies.

Then I remember the miniature being
who appeared at my shoulder once when I was resting
cape fluttering, arms out like Dogoda
tiny goddess of the west wind

my mother's and father's first-born
who because of their mourning
was a memory I was forbidden to share.

Gone nine years before my birthday
strangled by the umbilical cord
the lilac breath of my sister.

I don't know what they intended to name her.
I call her Phoebe, daughter of Gaea.
Phoebe would have peach fuzz like Mother
without the cigarette breath.

She would wear loose-weave wool skirts
have long arms and wisdom
and be my shepherdess.

I talk to Phoebe
I don't wait for an answer
I tell her everything
on my walks, in the car.

I tell her about Mother and her illness
about Dad surviving his way to death.
Everything.

Communing with Phoebe
I remember a photo of me
holding a small bag of copper hobby wire
resigned, unsmiling.

I put my arms around my neck
and comfort me.

## What Kind of Boy

*After Irene Rutherford McLeod's Lone Dog*

*You're a smart boy* my mother said
*Smart enough to know better* my father said
*Smarten up* my brother said like there was someone else to be.

I wanted to be a fast boy tough boy slick boy
hair all up in butch wax
duck's ass on the back of my head.

They weren't around long enough
to see whatever boy I would become
sky boy sly boy staggering boy falling boy.

*You could be Head Boy* my aunt Eunice said
Head Boy is a jock boy popular boy teacher's boy I am not that boy
I didn't trust her after that.

I am more of a gravel road boy daffodils boy
running down a portage trail
barbed wire scar by my left eye survival boy.

I find fresh money leaking from tall buildings treasure boy
piss four-hundred-ten feet off the J.L. Hudson Building
Friday night open 'til nine fountain boy raining boy.

I toss Welch's Grape Juice bottles out my aunt Eunice's
twenty-nine-story window whole long airy seconds
to hear the glass shatter on the flagstones heedless boy.

Star-Tribune old-timers slam their news copy
on the spike and cry out, *Boy.*
One of us comes running
errand boy.

The world allows
a dependable boy.
I got here on my own.

## Mr. Death

If I were to draw
back then right now
it would be a book
of crude black and white
cartoons of skeletons
and narrow faces

little stick figures
scurrying about
smoking cigarettes
eating canapés
making airline reservations.

My father vital
bridling with energy
cleans his briar pipe.
My mother beautiful
and sad in yellow cotton
walks slowly.

My brother, distant
oils his catcher's mitt.
I, in kinetic poses
rush from cookie jar
to *Dragnet* to *Danger Man*
to *Captain Kangaroo* how I hated you.

At their funerals back then
death was invisible, immutable.
I called it Mr. Death.

It lurked
like a mold
a recurring weather system
an unseen moon

a dark comic book hero
speaking backwards
counting down
to zero.

## The Clinic

My Aunt Ellie drives me to the clinic
snowdrifts flecked with asphalt
like black pepper on eggs
melting on the curb in the early morning sun.

The snow will re-freeze tonight
and leak more blackened weather
down the sewer tomorrow.

My Aunt Ellie has convinced my mother
I need to talk to someone other than her
and the rest of my aunties.
There is no one left but aunties.

The grandmas and grandpas have died
most of the uncles have passed on
and the ones who haven't have drifted away
like pine logs down the Mississippi River.

Even my mom is an auntie.
Maybe she is my auntie and not my mom.
What's the difference?
They all look the same.

Bottoms big as Buicks
breasts tented by sailcloth
and little flowers
like Spring Fling
at the Botanical Society.

I've had carnal with most of them
in my head anyway
a different auntie every morning
before I get dressed for work.

Sunday they all baked me something.
It is a plan they have
to make me zippy again
like in the old days they say
when I was a tiny child.

My Aunt Collie made a half-dozen Swedish croissants
a cream-colored excuse for dog snacks.
My Aunt Ellie baked me a half-dozen
oatmeal cookies hard as hockey pucks.

They take me to the gardens
and I nab those cookies and
skip them across Minnekawaga Pond
splish, splash, splash
like round rocks on Lake Superior
they angle their way down
to their deaths on the bottom.

Now Billy, how are they going
to clean those cookies
out of the pond?
asks my Aunt Ellie

Well, they could just turn
up the heat and boil them off
like mosquitoes, I say.

They don't have heat in the pond.
You remember the pond.
You used to put your little boats in it.

My Aunt Ellie's voice
is like a milk truck
spilled over in a gulley
with its engine idling.

My mom, or Aunt Mommy as I call her
made me a date pudding that stands up
like a penis on a puppy.

It just sits there on its plate
angry, shimmering, ready to attack.
I am afraid it is going to melt
and die in the grass
like a tiny child.

On the clinic wall a light goes on.
In a dark office Dr. Nelson
a cramped man
stubs out a cigarette
in a moose antler ashtray
and slides a stack of ink
blot drawings across his desk.

These are from Switzerland
like the chocolate, he says.
I'm going to show them to you one at a time.
You will tell me what you see.

He edges his chair toward me.
I stare down at the pages.
And words come out of me
like in a fast game of charades.

This picture is a dead bug
but he is comfortable now
his stripes are not clothing
they are nature's designs, I say.

Is he scary?
asks Dr. Nelson.
No. He's dead.

Rushing through the pictures
I say things like *stag, squashed, pointy.*
I figure the words are related to my thoughts
but I'm not embarrassed
I am happy someone is interested.

Are you all right for time? he asks.
I am confused by the question.
Time can be a bitter expanse
it yawns at me, cocoons me
propels me like a touch hole
at the end of a burning wick.

When does your school start? he asks.
I glance at my watch.
Well, I have to be standing in the hall
outside my office bright
and early at eight o'clock, I say.
I should go.

Yes, you should, he says.
A School Principal
can't be late to school
on a Monday morning.

**Keep Your Eye on the Ball**

I was five, my brother was ten.
My dad smacked a hardball right at me
I flinched and winced
I didn't even try to catch the freaking thing.

I thought this is big boy big man
baseball bat stuff
hard as dead cork.
Where is my place in this?

Keep your eye on the ball, my dad shouts.
I stand there holding my uncle Gerry's
old Chicago mitt oiled with
neetsfoot nearly to extinction.

I won't cry.
I know how to be a blur, a, shadow,
how to mock it up.
I watch like a study hall monitor.

My dad loves me more.
But he is playing for my brother.
Always trying to catch up on their thing
which is erratic.

There is a generosity to my dad
an anger to my brother.
And me? A sleight of hand.

My dad bunts with the Louisville Slugger
thirty-two ounces of hickory
bonk goes the hardball
careening off our soft pocked lawn.

Maybe my mom will bake something
that will stop this nonsense.

## Place Old Blade into Recess

My hand hides in my pocket like a mole down a tunnel. I run my fingers over smooth round corners of a box no bigger than a tin of matches, the switch slides like mercury, off, on, off, on, Detective Joe Friday on a *Dragnet* walkie-talkie.

*Did you have to give him that?* My mother says, *Make sure it's empty for God's sake. He's five years old. He'll slice his fingers off.*

The box is a gift from my father. I watch him shave. He flicks the switch, the blade emerges like a steel tongue, drops into his razor, he lathers up, glides through billows of foam, lips puckered, nose up, drags the blade over his throat past his sideburn, puffs out his cheeks like blowing a trumpet solo and rinses off.

Dabbing spots of blood with a styptic pencil he sprinkles his palm with St. John's Bay Rum, slaps his face with the good smell, tosses the empty dispenser in the trash. *Can I have that, Dad?* He gives me a look then fishes through the garbage and retrieves the tiny blue box. *Here you go, kiddo. Give 'em a rat-tat-tat and a good what for.*

My mother zips me up and sets me out on the back stoop. A late-summer Iowa sky, folds of clouds that never seem to go away hover over the railroad tracks and corn fields, a wind pushes at the tops of the trees. I raise the blue box to my lips: *Attention, attention, do you hear me?* Song sparrows dive straight down and level out next to me like they're listening.

## Mother and Father

Mother was a woman with a house on her head
weighed down by the walls and roof
a constitution like a sculpture
marbled, lithe
naked from the thighs down.
She had small feet.

Father recorded his thoughts
in tiny leather
notebooks.

Smug, self-identified, he told me
Making you with your mother
was like learning to tie a bow tie.
He was impatient and a little sad.

With your mother I was like Pierrot
ministering unto the Queen.
I preferred a woman with a sparrow
between her thighs
a woman agleam
a woman more like her photographs.

He said of her
I loved her then.
I miss her when I can.

## Mannequin

My Aunties took me to the Rose Garden, a tattered, sandy spot of paths and rusted signs which once identified bushes and shrubs that now overgrow the edges of the place. My mother's sisters smelled of coffee and drugstore cologne. They had fuzz on their upper lips, *lady-staches* my Aunt Collie called them.

Though my aunties were blood and comforted me when I was with them they felt as far away as billboards on a hill—gathered cotton skirts, old purses, their manner of speaking in low cigarette tones, small felt hats with folded veils and pearl hatpins, *this'll put a man's eye out,* my Aunt Collie said, feigning a lunge.

After a slow turn around the Garden my aunties drove me back to their rambling shingle house. *Oh, your mother,* they said with a sad downturn of voice. *Oh, your brother, what a handsome boy, how could he go like that?*

In the den my aunties kept a dress mannequin moldable in shape and size made from wire hexagons ringed together, its pubus naked, untended. It lived in a closet with house dresses and an ironing board. At the hips it was bolted to a walnut stand with wheels.

I pulled it out and turned its shoulders to me. She was headless, armless, legless but seemed proud of purpose, fitted with blouses, ensembles, pinned and stretched. Now naked, poised.

To soften the chafe and scratch I placed a tissue in the hole below her stomach and entered her. It was fast and complete. The stained tissue fell at my feet. I rolled her back into the closet and gently closed the door. She belonged to my aunties.

## Green Disappears

Gangster spooks toss me in the back of a musty old sedan
rolling fast and silent, the smell of dry cowhide and rusted steel.

We pass under a rusty portal to a ranch or castle or cemetery.
Headlights shine on hillsides of black spruce and hemlock.

Green disappears, empty bluffs of dusky clay, sulfur night iron.
We slow to a stop. They push me out.

I stand next to my brother's casket by a hill like the one where we sledded
where he loaned me quarters and we ate candy.

The thin gray lid of his coffin is loose. His green eyes are open.
He is impatient, angry, his face hooded in darkness.

The coffin lid falls apart in my hand
like bits of woodshop waste.

### Mars God of War

I, actor, born in a hall of linoleum
a line of jittery eight-year-olds
triumphant over all seven-year-olds
in Roman battle skirts and rusted helmets
like derbies on a row of cantaloupes.

Dimpled mothers' coats hang
over the backs of tired desks
as they wait for their pageant boys
my sword huge and heavy hooked
on my Lake Itaska beaded belt.

A roar in my head my line
my first and only shiny line
*I am Mars God of War*
will come soon loud as magma.

Like small heads of cattle we low
stand trim and stern I in character
wrists laced tight a daemon in bare feet.
Joggs McCann nudges me,
*Your turn.*

Leather and steel I stride on stage
hoist my sword like a mast in a squall
and with a wrong-handed swirl
knock a sandwich-sized chunk of yellow plaster
out of Miss Dewey's music room wall.

Gasps arise from the littles and the mothers
but not for a buggy second do I pause,
my tongue a high-board *I am Mars God of War.*
Breaths held, eyes unmoving
like dinghies in the calm.

Ka-thunk sprinkle sprinkle
the hunk of stucco and a spew of dust
settle on the floor synchronous
with my myth and power
followed by a dollop of applause.

## Imaginary Ring

Where sweating men in tights and mismatched colors charge at me,
mask their spinning eyes. Clerks, drivers, and men in suits
assume their roughie roles around the gallery of honor.

See the tiny fight the large left pummel right
the jagged brawl the broken road
*Las Luchas.*

On the Metro I stand, hating.
I resent eyes that will not meet me.
I am willing to be kidnapped even hung
by my ankles from an electric grid
if only someone will say,
*Forgive me, but I know you.*

I ask a stranger,
*Mind if I arouse your bag?*
*That's mine,* he snaps.
*It's safe with me,* I say,
*as long as you don't turn your back.*

His pock-marked head swivels
his skull narrows
his chin snaps like a gopher trap
I can smell his skin.

I have stepped through the mist
and feel so alive.
The train has no sound.
I think I've won.

*You don't know these people,*
my Aunt Eunice says at supper.
*I never hurt anybody,* I say.

She taps her forehead,
*The markings in your skull.*
*Things have roosted there*
*and left their rubbish spread about.*

She takes a scoop of turkey stuffing.
I finger for bones in my mouth.

## Rope

I haven't grown a plant
since that clot of cannabis
sprouted on my shingle roof
in summer near the Mississippi
by the elms and oaks.

Muscular skies grew this thing
a nervous grasshopper green
cardboard box sides broken by weather
the root ball reached
to the very edges of the dirt.

I tried to pull it up
amazed by its strength.
It had grown to its furthest extremity
the end of the soil
the start of the house.
I was unable to lift it.

**Killer Art**

*Cy Twombly is at MOMA,* my mother-in-law Sophie announced, *I'm going.* Sophie taught art in women's prisons. She got furloughs and bussed prisoners to the Met, the Frick, the Guggenheim. She strolled in, copper earrings silver bracelets clanking and glinting in the pinpoint spots.

I'd never seen Twombly's pale canvases of Latin words and clouds of blood in oil. I put on my readers, and on the lower corner of one canvas was a pale wash of gray. Twombly had drawn a graphite flock of tiny penises and buttocks squirting and shitting like what I drew on my eighth-grade Bible History workbook. I blurted out, *Cy Twombly draws dicks and ass.* A crowd gathered thinking I was a docent.

*Of course he does,* said Sophie. *He's known for that. All male artists do that.* At home in Yonkers Sophie showed me her students' work. On the back were stickers: Property of New York State Women's Prison System. *I bring these home,* she said, *otherwise the guards throw them out.* Above her medicine cabinet hung a painted plywood tiger. *She shot her husband,* Sophie said. *Did ten years for it. She was talented. As an artist.*

## Visitors

I sit on tubes rusted as alley cabbage
and wait for my wife to leave for work.
It's ten in the morning.

A man comes in says he's my nephew.
I offer him a drink.
When I'm flushed there's more to enjoy.

I twist my head, get a slappy sound.
A knock on the door, it's my agent
he loads me with kerosene
and asks if I have a match.

It's still ten in the morning.
Whiskey burns like a good fire
leaves my tongue unharmed.

Down below there's dull air
I want to hang me
but I don't want to get up.

Kentucky Tavern
the time of white lightning
I was younger then
drinks around.

At night my wife returns.
*What's on*, she asks.
*Re-runs of me,* I tell her.

TV pixels large as irises
electric grid
the odds of death
railroad tracks on fire.

I start the argument all over again.

## Jim's Radio & TV

*It's for you*, my father shouts
between smoked fish and raw onion.
I am Tarzan, telephone my vine,
I pick it up.

My friend John Waterhouse breathes fast
*Jim's TV & Radio just showed me how to solder*
*a microphone to a radio and I can hear my voice.*

At twelve we wanted nothing more than to be amplified,
lips osculating on an Electro-Vox 664 big bassy men.
On-air I could sell a war, chronicle the midnight disappearance
of an innocent family of four, brought to you by Chesterfield.

In a sooty corner storage room where coal once lay
rested a Philco Model 20 cathedral tube radio
that my father ignominiously painted Tiffany rose.

Once-lustrous walnut burl now cobwebbed
riven with woodworms, drowned in baby-ass pink,
my father's dry prickle of a brush lying to the side.

I unbolt the cover, wiggle the condenser,
resistors, transformer, to see if they will
light up the tubes.

This once tawny jewel
is silent, dark as a vault.
I fault my father's will to paint.

## Locker Room Talk

I am an unreliable
hardly a workman
a squatting mannequin with gum pink lips
I have no ideas about the world.

My friends look like Cate Blanchett
I introduce them as Dave
I'm out of cigarettes.

I freeway my hair with orange blossoms
I listen to the cry of chachalacas
the great kiskadee
dharma talk
I have to try.

As I preen before the mirror
I hear the piercing din of pasty televised mouths
guarded by armies no longer distant.

My shoulders hulk with ripsaw dust
my brow my throat.
Hidden in succulents beneath my window
a machete a chainsaw

Edged out of my torpor
I wander down the street toward
the scene of the sounding crime.

Under paving stones
beneath the worms
loathing is reborn
reptilian throats
masters of horror
Trumps.

Will I seek revenge
truck with strangers
march in black block balaclava
will I seek justice?

I keep thinking
I have a killer punch.
What if I miss.

## Saturnia

In a cab on my way to my mother's grave
in southwest Philly St. James Kingsessing
near the Schuylkill, acres of Colonial tombstones.

I ask the driver to stop for flowers
there are no florists on the way.
*How about M&Ms or Milk Duds*, he suggests.
Have a little respect
though I don't say it.

Out behind the sanctuary I sit on worn concrete steps.
Across the way through the rusted wrought iron fence
a family watches me.

In a blue volcanic pool
my mother afloat in blood-warm water
the odor of sulfur
glands of the earth.

I remember her breasts
civil, carefully lotioned
spoken for.

She flutter kicks
clouds of thermal moss
until I can't see her.

Any farther down she'll
be in an anteroom of hell.
This is as much mothering as I can handle.

**I am Zorro**

She made boxes out of boxes my favorite a diorama bathed in white enamel paint a Barbie Doll crashes through the cardboard roof like a naked one-armed Ninja empty speech bubbles hang like clouds from paper tabs.

The night she vanished with another man I found the white box dismantled like a defused bomb on the kitchen table where I made her French toast and apple salad. A clue at a crime scene Barbie, ripped from the roof, lies face down, her tiny plastic finger pointing to a cartoon bubble that reads *Help*, a one-word goodbye, *help*.

I lie in bed and talk with my lover's imaginary body. I dream of her olive hair. I cry like a house-husband. To calm myself I spend an evening at the theater. An actress steps down from the stage and washes my feet. I luxuriate in her warmth, her hands, her eyes. I am certain that long ago she and I touched tongues in Unitarian Church School. *I remember* she says.

At her apartment I lay open my heartsick story of cloaked motives and murky twists. *I think you've got some things to work out* she says.

The next day at school my seventh-graders and I write sonnets together. We stage battles from the War of the Roses. We act out big ideas. I am not just a school teacher I am an artist a philosopher. I am masked and mustachioed I wear a black satin cape I am Zorro. With my sword I carve a gaping wounding Z into a bad man's flesh.

## Dream Visits with My Father

I.

I visit my father in his carriage house.
He sits reading the newspaper in his old yellow leather chair
held together with brass upholstery tacks that shine like teeth.

The view out his window is a sugar sunset tossed into a violet sky.
It has been a while since we talked.
He still doesn't seem to have time.


II.

He decides to pay me a visit.
He pulls up in his sea green Packard
rolls down the window
and tells me how proud he is of me.

I am happy to see him but I have to run off
to do some heroic thing or other.
I tell him I will be right back.

When I return eager to talk
he has gone.
I hurry off to our old house.

Only the foundation is visible
the bare outline
dusted over
by the passage of time.

**Try My Luck**

When I climb steps I count down
like at a rocket launch
increasing my odds of survival.

When I was eight I was afraid of being kidnapped.
At thirteen I was angry as fate mistook me
for an orphan Bozo Bop Bag.

An all-knowing coven watched me
through the wall with smirks of bemusement
and grudging respect for the fact that I've even made it this far.

To mourn those who are gone
and to taste revenge
I watch *Fast & Furious* and I cry.

I look for hidden meanings in incidental moments
I open a door and conjure up a man across the lake
enormous nostrils, jut jaw, taking aim at me.

If I stop and breathe and take in the view
it's only a gun glued shut with rust and time.
It's like that between me and the world.

Trucks won't heel over and plunge into rivers
trains won't dragon up into the sky
babies won't tumble into the gap beyond the platform.

I am perfectly intact
like my front gate latch
which simply needs tightening.

## Wabash Banner Blue

A night of trees and winds
mangled sparrows
a dreamless sleep

a shutter opens
nursing in brumal air
moans of the slowing Wabash train
a stretch of Pullman cars

the house cracks
all is weightless
distant breathing

out my window
coiled on the lawn
a behemoth with a witch's purse
a sack of stunned blood in a thicket.

I must not stir I must not look
I must not wander on this night.
Damn the ones who taught me
*If I should die before I wake.*

To alarm the daemon I clap like a blowout, sing arias,
scuttle down the stairs to the steak knife drawer.
Careful not to rouse the creature's eye I flee the house.

At the edge of the wood a skeleton rises shrieking Emergo!
Skeletons don't scare me
I sniff for meat,
bullets don't scare me
I survived one for my mother's breast
one for my brother's kidneys
one for my father's heart.

And they will aid me now.
I scale the cemetery wall,
at my father's grave
I kick aside a clump of grass.

In the ground on a Bible-sized stone
my stepmother's name
her oblivion, her coffee cup reeking of whiskey
all the good cooking and car rides.
I didn't save her jewelry
I sold it for blow.

My father died on his stairlift
a copy of *The Raven* in his lap.
I pulled him down, laid him out
and breathed into his blue mouth,
nothing but the sound of soup inside him.

I want to hear his voice
his South Chicago twang
the word *car* as hard as ore
I want to sleep in his bed
he might call at a late hour.

My mother's grave surrounded
by old stones of family I never knew,
I see her, the vividness of her
bubbles of mercury
the green flash.

A cavernous scream slashes the air
behemoth on the graveyard floor
pulses its stunted wings.

If fate rips me like a leaf
I have made arrangements with my family.
In that final blaring moment
throttled by monster death
my mind will make myth

and I will see them all again.
They will gather in a sleeping car
aboard the Wabash Banner Blue
gingerly pull closed my compartment door
my fear of monsters and the dark no more.

## Man Talking

My father's business suits twist down the toilet, crisp summer linens, Glasgow flannels, Donnegal tweeds, a dank swirl of sartorial waste. Kneeling on the flooded master bath tiles dredging for his waterlogged wardrobe my father hisses, *there is not an ounce of man in you. You need decorum.*

We engage in a brief scuffle I catch him with a bolo punch to the crown he phones the cops and has me committed. It's a kind of ritual we have in our house like spring cleaning.

In the hospital a car cigarette lighter is mounted on the wall by the nurses' station where pyromaniacs melt wax on their bottoms and light their pubic hair on fire. Visitors Day my parents wear badges with photos of their faces.

*That's not necessary,* I say, *I know who you are,* (cartoon donkeys pushing warm clouds out their breezies.)

My mother informs me she's dropped out of child-rearing class. My father hands me a tiny evergreen tree made of felt. *It's a puppet,* he says slipping it over his finger and growling like a pirate, *Walk the plank,* his eyes a pair of life-ring buoys floating at sea.

When he and I argue my mother usually cries. This time she just scrubs something off her blouse with a handkerchief. She loves pretty clothes. She has bulbous Russian breasts like the domes on Saint Basil's Cathedral.

*We're taking you home,* my father says handing me a lunch basket. My meds have kicked in my fears of the moist outdoors the grey sun the day have merged into a restive corner. My parents walk me to the car. I stare up at the linen sky, thickets of leaves hover capable of striking out at me.

I say to no one in particular, *Is my sex attached to my skeleton?* My mother begins to cry. My father spits out the car window, *Look, son, drink from the fleshy part of the passion fruit. That's what men do when we're thirsty.*

I shout back, *When you're thirsty you visit Aunt Ellie in her condo and lap up her hidden waters under her brushed silk duvet.*

Mother rolls down the window and calls my father her dirty old saint. *Thank God for men,* she says. *My doctor thinks I lack friends, but who needs them when I have the two of you?*

## Emily

Emily the cat
sitting on a tractor beam
turns her calico head to face me.
She is nearly gone.
I cry for her as for my mother.

When my mother died I asked my father
what happens in a crematorium
picturing her in a sun yellow nightgown
lying silent, still,
flames reach up
blue and fire brown.

My father took a coach-class flight
alone to Philadelphia
carrying a box wrapped in baker's twine
my mother's ashes
an angel food cake.

The lake place we rented
after mother was gone
had no-see-ums
that crawled through screens
and high-humidity
between bays and stands of pine.

Mother was long ago.
Emily was only recent.
Her warm eyes regarded me
with directness, curiosity
a slow blink

saying I trust you enough,
to close my eyes
and open them again to you.

We keep her ashes
and her plaster paw print
on the bookshelf in the bedroom.

## Bagni

Thick slavic legs
lycra tucked in body folds
hair bunched in caps
preparation for the waters.

I inhale the steam
into cranial recesses
in one yawning sigh.

Genial competition begins
for places along the edge.
There is a decorum.

A man's wife glides by,
pale bosoms
soft speckled skin
I imagine she nursed a child.

I dip my head to see her trim gold legs
as she pedals the pool
her steps sure as coral.

There is nothing so intimate
as a stranger's body
near you in the water.

Her husband in violet spandex
clutches the tiles
doodles in body squiggles
submarine squats.

She floats, a parade of flowers
the water endows her
with a rippling grace.

No Roman fresco gives such measure
to the slow spinning of flesh
circling in the lens of the waters.

## SC Verdugos

Beware a wayward ball
floating between men
the bladder of a goat
a living thing *la pelota.*

Tommy second striker lopes across the AstroTurf
claps hands and without ceremony the game begins.
*Open up we open up* the coach rags like a bulldog.

*Keep up the pressure keep up the pressure*
as if yelling it twice makes it clearer.
Tommy dances backwards like down a stairway.

Knocked sideways he lands on his belly
pops up and does a robot mime,
a spectator says, *Dude his last game was what?*

Announcer in a red headset chants
play-by-play to a smartphone on a tripod
warbling, *Ay, ay, ay, ay, canta y no llores.*
Men in the stands giggle, *Do they hire somebody?*

Palms on hips Tommy pounds his head into the ball
jaws slam to a curved air kick.
*Puto, puto,* a bald man yells
hiding his mouth with his hat.

Kick run wait minute quarter half.
The ball in a slow dim arc breezes
to the sideline and grounds out.
*Ain't no winners just you losers.*

Spiked feet chop at the turf like cleavers.
A minute to go Tommy takes it in the gut arms out
Superman flying by a green screen
and drops like a pig, you can hear the air go out of him.

So comes the endgame stroll in spikes and stripes
shoulders sag eyes wander they tag all hands
like they're banging shut a locker.

## Underbrush

Our love was fiction read aloud at night
drug smoke on stark white days
black forest leather draped her cuffs
a neck of curls a perfumed art.

Psychotropic tablets on our tongues
we wandered for a day
that would not be what I imagined.

It stripped me to a boy lost and fearful
she a graceful thin-lipped mermaid in gold lamé
diving down to haunt the sea.

I crawled in buckthorn and coyote brush
alongside ticks, ants, and hag moths.

*Let's take a warm bath,* she suggested.
I dragged myself out
awash in earth and twigs.

We sat on straight-backed chairs
with cigarettes like cardboard
our clawfoot tub a rusted creek
of old bathers and common debt

then slid down in water
cold as blue granite
and clutched our knees
like punished children.

Hours stalked by
at the end of which she left
wearing that leather coat.

The uptick
the downdraft
all of my making.

## Inventory

*Have you ever experienced dizziness?*
On occasion
first kiss
Camel straights
inner ear.

*Have you ever had visions of grandeur?*
I've never wanted to be famous
I think it's dangerous.

*Have you ever had depressive episodes?*
No. I mean, sure.
Once I cried in a toilet stall with my arms spread wide
holding the gray metal walls apart
about Janet who left me for Darren
on Spring break in Fort Lauderdale.

*If you found a significant amount of cash on a bus would you turn it over to the driver?*
No.

*Have you ever considered suicide?*
Not seriously, no.

*Have you ever thought about homicide?*
I wonder about young men and projectiles
finger guns and cowboys
concentrated fire and gun shows
Sandy Hook, Orlando, Las Vegas,
Parkland, Baghdad.

*How do you feel about spiders?*
They deserve a chance.

## Milk and Hyacinth

I was taught by a man
in clingy cottons and sneakers
the salt scent of the asanas.

Today my teacher is jeweled
winnowed, a palimpsest.

She strides like flying
with the grace of an Echo Park dove
aiming, calling softly
slowing hearts.

Sure weather
her voice in petals
rhythm, history
gravity works well with her.

To mirror, to keep left from right
she describes milk and hyacinth
*Tadasana, Trikonasana.*

She aids our breath
our speed our strength
she leaves no one behind.

With her this day
I witness perfection of us
the practice of body magic
since before she could sit.

She is she and not of me
she in yoga grace
is my daughter
my child
my master.

**B**ill **Ratner** is a *Poets & Writers* Readings & Workshops Grant recipient. His audio performances are featured on National Public Radio's *Good Food, The Business,* and KCRW's *Strangers;* he is a 9-time winner of The Moth Story Slams. His poems, essays, and stories are published in *The Chiron Review, The Baltimore Review, Rattle Magazine's Rattlecast, Pleiades, KYSO Flash, South Florida Poetry Journal, Rat's Ass Review, Nixes Mate, Willawaw Journal, Missouri Review Audio,* and other journals. He is the author of *Familius Books' Parenting for the Digital Age: The Truth Behind Media's Effect on Children*, an Indie Excellence Book Award winner. As a voice actor he is heard on movie trailers, computer games, Cartoon Network, Smithsonian Channel, History, Discovery, Netflix, FX Channel, etc. Info at: http://billratner.com/author • @billratner

CPSIA information can be obtained
at www.ICGtesting.com
Printed in the USA
BVHW031657100721
611576BV00004B/506